Lipman Pike
America's First Home Run King

This **PJ BOOK** belongs to

_____

_____

Pj Library®

JEWISH BEDTIME STORIES and SONGS

By Richard Michelson
and Illustrated by Zachary Pullen

Lipman Pike hated to stand still. From behind the cashbox he shook out his left leg, and then his right.

The bell above the door jingled. Lip glanced toward his older brother, but Boaz was studying in the back room and didn't even look up.

"Good day, Mrs. Kaufman," Lip's father said. Mr. Pike was always polite. The neighbors called him "a real gentleman."

"*Goede dag*," Mrs. Kaufman said. She had met Lip's father years ago on the boat that had brought them to America from Holland. Sometimes she still spoke Dutch. "My son is in need of …"

Lip leaped into action. It was 45 feet to the front window display. Ninety feet round trip: exactly the distance between home plate and first base. Lip could run it in 14 seconds. He grabbed a package and raced head down. He heard fast-moving footsteps behind him and looked up in time to see Boaz slam a pair of boy's stockings on the counter.

"The best service in the city!" Mr. Pike announced proudly. "My boys could beat a racehorse in the home stretch."

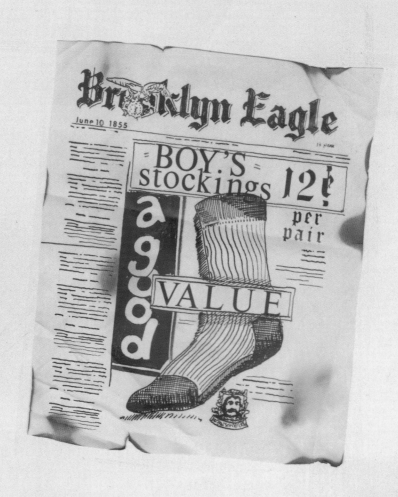

"I finished my bar mitzvah homework," Boaz told his father, as he and Lip headed toward the door. "Can we go watch the men play Base?"

It seemed like everybody in Brooklyn was playing this exciting new game. Each neighborhood club had a team and even some of the Jewish boys would practice batting and throwing when their parents weren't watching.

"Not my sons!" Mrs. Pike complained to her husband. "If grown lads chased after a leather ball in Europe, people would call them childish. Boaz is almost a man, and when Lip finishes his chores, he should exercise his mind."

"I won't let Base interfere with the boys' education," Mr. Pike promised his wife. "But in America even the smartest young men chase balls like silly boys. We want our children to fit in with their neighbors, not to live like foreigners in their birthplace."

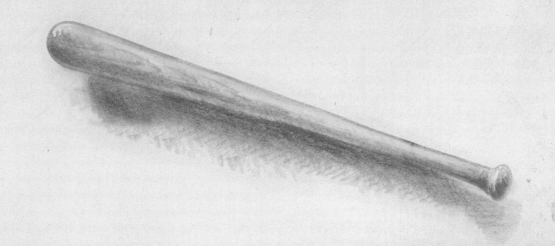

Some evenings, after Mr. Pike locked the shop door, the boys would quickly dust the shelves and sweep the floors. Then Boaz would toss jawbreaker candies down the center aisle as Lip swung the broom handle, and raced around the store.

Now, three years later, and only seven days after his own bar mitzvah, Lip followed Boaz to a local junior club meeting.

"Sure, he's young and left-handed," Boaz told his teammates, "but he's as fast as a racehorse and as strong as one, too."

"No one can outrun a racehorse," the team captain said to Boaz, "but if he is half as fast as you, that is good enough for me."

Lip was invited to join the junior club and play in his first official amateur match.

A couple of ladies in lawn chairs were picnicking in the park and their young sons were climbing nearby trees, but Lip imagined that everybody in Brooklyn was preparing to watch the match. He felt butterflies rise in his stomach and his knees go weak.

"Don't worry," Boaz reassured his brother. "In my first match I didn't get a single hit."

Lip wondered if that was supposed to make him feel better, but as he stepped up to the plate, he forgot all about being nervous, and he hit the first pitch high over the right fielder's head.

As the years passed, word of Lip's batting power and speed spread throughout Brooklyn. Customers would shop at the haberdashery just to talk about Base.

The store prospered. "That's what good manners, fast service, and honest prices will do," Mr. Pike told his wife. "Of course," she answered, "it helps that every lad in town wants to purchase his stockings from Lip."

When Lip turned 21, he told his parents he was moving to Philadelphia to play for the Athletics. Mr. Pike was worried. "Where will you work?" he asked. "Here, business is good. I can pay you $2 a day."

"You traveled halfway around the world to follow your dreams," Lip reminded him. "There is nothing I love more than Base." Then Lip waved his parents closer and whispered. "The Athletics' captain offered me $20 each week to play for his club."

Mrs. Pike shook her head in disbelief. "Who ever heard of anyone being paid to chase a ball?" she asked.

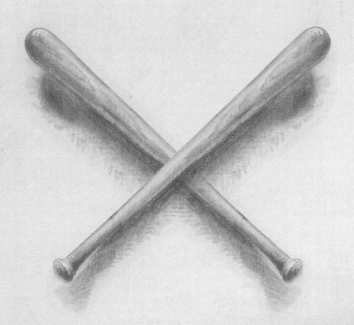

That year the Athletics won 23 matches and only lost twice. In one match Lip hit six home runs. He was their best player.

But the other club members all came from the same hometown, and they began to grumble when it was rumored that Lip was being paid.

"It's unfair," the second baseman said. "Who ever heard of a *professional* ballplayer? Only a working man should get wages."

"Besides," the left fielder added, "I hear that Pike's a Jew. How can we trust him when we play against Brooklyn?"

Lip was voted off the team.

But Lip refused to give up his dream.

He joined the New Jersey Irvingtons until a man named Boss Tweed invited him to play closer to home. Lip was excited because the New York Mutuals were one of the best clubs in the league.

"Of course, we can't pay you," Boss Tweed explained. "That would be against Base Ball Association policy and, as New York's Commissioner of Public Works, I would never break the rules." He waved Lip closer so he could whisper. "But I can offer you a job in our government office at Tammany Hall. You would have little work to do and plenty of time to play ball."

"All the best players are getting paid these days," Lip told his mother. He'd just arrived home after the season ended.

"The *Eagle* says that there is going to be a professional league," Lip's father said. He waved the newspaper excitedly.

Lip smiled. "That is what I was about to tell you," he said. "I was asked to be the captain of the Troy Haymakers."

Lip traveled to Troy to practice with his new teammates. "Sure, we're all professionals," he heard one player whisper, "but Lip grew up in Brooklyn, and I hear that he's a Jew. How can we be sure of his loyalty? How can we trust him when we play his old team in New York?"

On May 25, 1871, the Haymakers entered Brooklyn's Union Grounds to play the heavily favored New York Mutuals. It seemed like everybody in the city had paid 50 cents to cheer for their team. Five thousand "cranks" were crowding into the ballpark. A thousand more fans lined up outside the fence.

"Only in America would people spend money to watch grown men chase after a ball," Mrs. Pike said to her husband, as she settled onto the ladies' bench.

"Only in America!" a familiar voice called out. It was Mrs. Kaufman waving from the next row.

"*Goede dag*, Mrs. Pike," she said. "This match I wouldn't miss for the world. Your Lipman is as fast as a racehorse and a real gentleman too, just like his father."

A reporter for the *Brooklyn Daily Eagle* was writing notes nearby. "No one can outrun a racehorse," he yelled out, "but if anyone could it would be Lipman Pike."

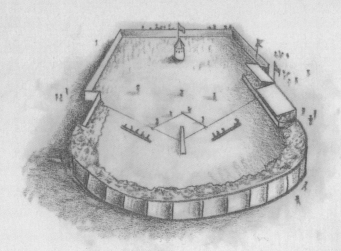

Lip looked out into the grandstand. He felt butterflies rise in his stomach, but as he stepped up to the plate, he forgot about being nervous, and he hit the first pitch high over the right fielder's head.

And the crowd cheered!

The Rest is History

Lip had six hits that day and the Haymakers won the match 25 to 10. By the end of the season, Lip tied for the league lead in home runs.

The following year Lip moved to Baltimore to join the Yellow Stockings. Once again he led the league in home runs.

On August 16, 1873, Lip proved that he could outrun a racehorse. Four hundred people paid 25 cents each and crowded into Newington Park in Baltimore to watch Lip beat a trotting horse named Clarence in a hundred-yard sprint.

In 1877 Lip, who had been nicknamed "the Iron Batter," hit his most famous home run when he struck a ball nearly 360 feet with enough power that it bent a metal rod atop a 40-foot-high pagoda in deep center field of the Union Grounds. That year Lip again led the league in home runs.

Lip retired in 1881 and opened a haberdashery in Brooklyn. He offered honest prices, fast service, and good manners. The store prospered. Everyone wanted to talk baseball and buy their stockings from Lipman Pike.

Lip was 48 years old when he died of heart disease on October 10, 1893. His funeral was attended by politicians from Tammany Hall, old teammates, many fans, and friends from Brooklyn's Jewish community.

The Sporting News noted that "Lip" Pike was "one of baseball's greatest sluggers" and "one of the baseball players ... who was always gentlemanly, both on and off the field."

Author's Note

Children were hitting, throwing, and catching balls well before the official game of baseball was developed, but in 1845 (the year Lipman Pike was born) a committee from the New York Knickerbockers Base Ball Club drew up a set of rules that helped change a child's game into a sport played by adults. Other clubs soon formed their own teams, and in 1858, the year of Lip's bar mitzvah, the National Association of Base Ball Players was formed. The league had 16 clubs, eight of which were from Brooklyn, six from across the river in Manhattan, and two from upstate. Baseball was a game of "amateurs," which meant that all the players had other jobs, and they played baseball for fun when they were not working. By necessity, therefore, players played for clubs near their homes.

During the Civil War, many of the Brooklyn boys played baseball in the army camps and the game began to spread throughout the country. But as baseball became America's most popular pastime, and spectators began to be charged to watch a "match" (game), "captains" (managers), hoping to both give their team an advantage and draw more "cranks" (fans), began to secretly pay some of the better players, even though it was against the rules.

There is no way of knowing which player was the first paid in this manner, but in 1866, when he was 21 years old, Lip accepted $20 a week to move from Brooklyn to Philadelphia to join the Athletics. When this was alleged in the local newspaper, Lip was ordered to appear before the NABBP governing committee. The charge was dropped, most likely because other players were being paid as well and other clubs were also guilty. But Lip became known as the first "professional" baseball player. Within two years the rules were changed and players were permitted to accept payment. This eventually led to the formation of the first all-professional league in 1871.

Lipman Pike grew up at a time when a small but growing wave of Jews was leaving Europe to come to America. While some came for political and religious reasons, most were hoping for greater economic opportunities. America was mostly welcoming, as it was becoming urbanized, and wanted immigrants who could read (which most Jews could do) and who had experience as merchants (which was one of the few occupations available to Jews in Europe). Organized anti-Semitism was not a major concern, as the number of Jewish immigrants was miniscule compared to the number of Irish and German immigrants. At the time of Lip's bar mitzvah, almost half of Brooklyn's population was foreign born. After the Civil War, however, Jews began to be singled out for not "fitting in." Emanuel Pike, Lip's father, encouraged his sons to assimilate by becoming involved in the new national pastime, while still retaining pride in their Jewish identity.

"LIP" PIKE

In memory of John Baldwin—always gentlemanly.
—RICHARD

The author wishes to acknowledge the following people for their gracious consultation:
Natalie Blitt, John Bowman, Rabbi Samuel Cohon, Peter Horvitz, Jonathan Sarna,
Robert H. Schaeffer, and James E. Young.

And special thanks to my editor, Aimee Jackson,
for her enthusiasm, advice, and friendship.

✳
✳✳

For every parent who plays catch with their kids.
—ZAK

Text Copyright © 2011 Richard Michelson
Illustration Copyright © 2011 Zachary Pullen

Sleeping Bear Press

315 E. Eisenhower Parkway, Ste. 200
Ann Arbor, MI 48108
www.sleepingbearpress.com

© Sleeping Bear Press

Printed and bound in the United States

10 9 8 7 6 5 4 3 2 1

Library of Congress Cataloging-in-Publication Data

Michelson, Richard.
Lipman Pike : America's first home run king / written by Richard Michelson;
Illustrated by Zachary Pullen.
p. cm.
ISBN 978-1-58536-465-7
1. Pike, Lipman, 1845-1893—Juvenile literature. 2. Baseball players—United
States—Biography—Juvenile literature. 3. Jewish baseball players—United
States—Biography—Juvenile literature. I. Pullen, Zachary, ill. II. Title.
GV865.P55M53 2011
796.357092—dc22
[B]
2010032367